De Corde Verba

Common Sense Haiku in
5-7-5 Beats

By
William Armstrong

Seeming to fall flat
Flat is the best to stand on
To gain our balance

We grow much larger
At the base of the mountain
Whose summit is love

Learning from error
We must make our own mistakes
Help when you need to

Our fat from the fire
Burning in embarrassment
Help us understand

What is the reason?
Why does everything go flat?
Help us see the seem

Rescue animals
Give them a house, safe and sound
Life is quid pro quo

Frail and fragile things
Like porcelain and crystal
Vulnerable beings

I'm hurt and get slammed
Pounded by pain and panic
All nature feels it

Nature by degrees
Growth covers all, slow and steady
Frail, old as when young

Book learn all you can
Smart is not the same as wise
Learn wisdom from life

Eyes open, mouth shut
Sounds abrupt and commanding
Helps us absorb life

What is our purpose?
Is there a reason we're here?
Don't think it, live it

If you must despair
Then the greatness of humankind
Should be your reason

Deluded thinking
Like a stagnant river flow
Is clouded by silt

Are objects all one?
Or, are they separate pieces?
How do you see them?

Envy shapes itself
Cheering others' misery
The shape of sadness

To stand tall when low
Valor is courage moving
Brave action moving

Raise your standard high
Your flag should be your heart-sign
Emblazoned by love

It's a simple task
To fight the good fight, is all
Call it our mission

It's variation
Our differences make us great
Love the dissimilar

Seek diversity
You'll find that fusion is slow
We should not be pure

See us as all one
Love our disparate cultures
Global family

Do not seek beyond
Keep grounded in now
Let the after be

Ask the great questions
Use them to know yourself well
Don't fear the answers

Vacation to learn
Not only to shop and drink
View the wider world

Talking is easy
Knowing is more difficult
The sign of wisdom

Teach them common-sense
Our kids have a right to know
Teach by example

How do we do it?
Live according to nature?
To ours, or the worlds?

Be like a runner
Start at the start, end when done
The race is finite

Teach more Earth-science
Show children how it started
Helps them keep it well

To know ourselves
To know what we do and why
A reason we're here

We feed on ourselves
We are sustained by our pride
Instead of our hearts

I should obey you
You do not obey nature
How can you lead me?

Nature teaches us
We should learn her example
Still our quick anger

We know our details
Money, hobbies, attractions
We don't know our mind

How long do we have?
Gaining but never seeing
How long does it last?

Alpha, omega
This life is a finite stretch
Correct the middle

We must have the best
The best food for our bodies
What about our minds?

Our flesh is a house
Be sure to furnish it with
The best furniture

Fundamental truths
Humanity and justice
Do not know borders

Peace calls it murder
But, because of a border,
War calls us hero

Do you want comfort?
Stop pursuing happiness
You'll find enjoyment

Temporary smile
Happiness is transient
Seek comfort instead

The search can frustrate
Losing it can leave anger
Let happiness go

Settle for comfort
A relaxed and easy life
Excitement will fade

You will search for fun
If you must, then do it well
Be well and stay safe

How to look forward
You have to forgive yourself
Each of us will err

Should you forgive me?
I have harmed you, so, myself
Forgive only you

Forgiveness is right
There is someone to forgive
That 'someone' is you

Someone hurt you bad
Give the gift of forgiveness
Then, go on your way

Pursue your success
But, don't hope others will fail
Defeat, don't destroy

Success is desired
There's nothing wrong with winning
We try harder then

Sometimes we increase
We add to our life and self
When we should decrease

Lose what you don't need
Leave the unnecessary
What's unessential?

Treat real friends as gems
They are rare and enrich us
Their value is love

We don't fall in love
Someone lifts us to its heights
And lets us live there

Sharing problems helps
I've never known anyone
Without a lifefull

Where does peace reside?
Must we live in a vacuum?
Only within us

Dreaming is success
Not having dreams to pursue
Is a life stagnant

Our circumstances
They do not decide for us
How happy we are

Don't scream at the dark
Do not stumble in blindness
Let hope be your light

Be just like a child
When they are just starting out
They love everyone

What is true evil?
When we can't focus on love
Then does evil win

To those in our lives
Not all deserve our respect
At least be polite

Love what you don't get
Sometimes, not getting your wish
Means we learn something

Treat love as a car
Check the oil and fuel gauges
Then step on the gas

Choose a goal in life
Then raise the roof of your dreams
As high as you can

Who chooses your mood?
Is it your circumstances?
You alone must choose

Throw away your plans
And get ready to live life
That's the way it goes

Let peace and calm win
In this battle we call 'Life"
Serene victory

To help your brain work
Don't live for adrenaline
Relax and slow down

Excitement is fine
Its pursuit will never end
If that's all there is

Remember this, then
To avoid criticism
Do nothing at all

Some say talk is cheap
It's the cheapest gift there is
Pay the price instead

Give all that you can
Keep in step with changing life
You'll get what you want

Know what a smile is?
The best plastic surgery
You'll never pay for

If you're impatient
In any great endeavor
See it fade away

Revel in your growth
But, don't expect others to
Their eyes may be closed

Plan to be content
Write it on your calendar
Then, make it happen

Try and force your way
You trample the porcelain
Gentle is the key

Love your excuses
With them, you cannot accomplish
They keep your days free

All that's possible
Will someday be accomplished
Are you the one who…

Turn your eyes inward
You are the greatest teacher
Of your life lessons

If you are content
Suddenly, everything fits
Into your life plan

Ask 'How?' don't ask 'Why?'
When it comes to reaching out
And helping others

Life is worth living
How do I know this is true?
I make it a fact

Your soul is your food
Learn to dine as a gourmet
Love as the main dish

Safety is our search
We look for a protector
You are your own knight

Share some of your soul
Help us see our human selves
Be more than a beast

Use your confidence
But, make sure it's not ego
There's a difference

Sometimes, messy's good
It shows us we can relax
Less to worry on

Peace is not the end
It is a constant process
An ongoing goal

We look to nature
Even those in the city
To remind us all

A heavy burden
I don't look to lighten it
Just for stronger arms

Treat all people with
Justice and benevolence
If you seek to lead

World peace starts at home
We must love our own world first
Comfort, peace and strength

The effort is all
Winning comes with effort first
Work is your first goal

Truth about yourself
Know your faults and fails
Then tell us of ours

You're lucky in love?
Then, fall in love everyday
With the same person

How do you know it?
How do you know it's for real?
It's new, everyday

So, it is failing
You sure your love is fading
Love or excitement?

Love of another
This should be a gift for us
Don't make it a need

Don't write down your goals
You'll need a big eraser
Make them part of you

The answer's simple
Like the search of the cosmos
It is what it is

Loves lives equally
Begin to love prejudice
And love disappears

Yesterday's stumble
Confessed in love and action
Shows wisdom today

Silence in its turn
And speaking when it's timed right
Is wisdom possessed

A daily fresh start
Awakening to new dawns
Life's recurring gifts

See the wrath you feel
Take some deep, refreshing breaths
Then course your action

Opportunity
Turned golden in ill fortune
Shows true astuteness

Fluid be your mind
Let your goals be loosely held
You'll stunt frustration

To fail is a step
Towards finding the right path
Where we find success

To see one's life scoffed
Yet to remain calm and kind
Shows where wisdom lives

Mistake sloth for love
Ignore action to find ease
You'll see life crumble

Know more your own faults
And point them out to yourself
But not in others

Maturity makes
Wisdom, love, care and concern
One's philosophy

To be full certain
Of any of life's actions
Is true court true doubt

Stumbling can help us
It wakes us when we sleep walk
And helps to guide us

Doing is progress
To know when to act or not
Stems from true wisdom

Happy is fleeting
Like all feelings, it flies fast
Be content instead

Hurricane feelings
When past, can leave us empty
And make us addicts

If you want too much
You will progress more than if
You possess too much

A dream. Life's painting
Brush stroke by brush stroke
Forms a masterpiece

What we leave our kids
Is either the quest for wealth
Or the search for wisdom

Don't paint for the blind
Nor compose for the deaf
Wisdom for the wise

To glut is discord
Neither too many nor few
Sing moderation

Don't deny too much
To starve is to watch life fly
We are consumers

Be part of the view
Life is a kaleidoscope
Move with the turning

A smirk can hide pain
A longing for something else
Which hopes abandons

Penetrate the fog
See to the center of things
The light of the wise

'What is the answer?'
Is not as important as
'What is the question?'

Start with epic fail
Search, quest, wonder, question, find
End with epic gain

Worry when you should
When not to means the world's end
So, when should we fret?

Stargaze now and then
Look up from the road ahead
As a reminder

Brach of public trust
Flaunt your mistake to the press
Loss of confidence

A small, thin error
Don't see it as a mistake
View the end success

Pounding waterfall
A thunder of life and sound
How does it calm me?

Accept your failings
Do your best to correct them
You'll accept other's

Many ways to see
Our global community
So small and fragile

Calm yourself right now
We act like naughty children
Sit down and be still

All the world's wisdom
If heeded by everyone
Could bullet-proof life

Don't hate misfortune
Do you want to stay a child?
We grow through ill-luck

A fool often says
"Because you can't disprove me,
You must believe me."

Don't fear the midnight
Of ignorance's horror-trek
Light is soon nearby

Wait for wonderful,
You'll find the wait wasteful
Love today's treasures

I long for love's balm
To dilute wisdom's coldness
Can they co-exist?

Act now, when you must
Action beats a soul's promise
To wait is to miss

A torrent of force
A hurricane of movement
Details in action

Thinking rules us all
Sometimes we need instinct too
To act without thought

Patience does blanket
All who view it in action
With a peaceful calm

Love is number one
The engine of life's progress
Wisdom is second

Let your mind run wild
Treasure your flights of fantasy
But, grasp the anchor

Don't school me too much
Can you heed your own advice?
Do you need it more?

Stand down and silent
Foolish advice giver, you
Mine is not to hear

Let me advise you
Even though I need it more
This is just ego

Sweet, loving concern
Always holding close to heart
Lessons of caring

'bye to yesterday
What did we know anyway?
Learn its lessons past

Don't cry for 'once was'
What 'once was' will be again
Treasure it this time

Love your possessions
They make a great soul's anchor
Feel them weigh you down

As the years tick past
Learn great lessons to pass along
Don't just get older

Who smiles in distress?
Those with wise maturity
Strive to be like them

When you are fatigued
Remember these two sure cures
Laugh and lots of sleep

What does make you laugh?
If it is something hurtful
It is not the cure

Laugh at someone else
Because they want you to laugh
This helps both of you

Move you smile muscles
It helps to remind us how
Use them or lose them

Beware false laughter
Laugh when you feel humor
Not just to make noise

Laugh just to make noise
You are robbed of the subtle
Joy real laughs can bring

The eyes can reflect
When a smile is real or not
More than the mouth does

Opinions are like
Armpits. All of us have them
And most of them stink

You must curb your views
You should know when to voice them
And when to be still

Do you believe it?
Or do you want to sound smart?
Silence is the best

Yours is a big world
How much of it do you know?
Always more to learn

Read all history
Know from whence we came till now
We are but a blink

See all around you
Hear with everything you have
These gifts go too fast

Take it for granted
But, remember to slow down
And appreciate

Full of energy
Movement is what we should be
But slow down to rest

Life's a hurricane
We live in a blast furnace
Learn to still your scream

Reign in your torrent
The eye of the hurricane
Make the eye your home

Search through the ruins
Find the answers to the 'why'
Human culture search

We are compassion
Empathy and sympathy
Holding others up

Look at your neighbor
Do you want to understand?
Look in the mirror

You care for others
Those in your circle, you love
Expand you circle

A helper for hurts
Cotton, stitches, bandages
Be a first aid kit

Love is not needed
If you want to help others,
Care is all you need

The pain of skinned knees
Stinging, burning and bleeding
The same for us all

"I love everyone"
These three words contain power
Show off your power

Compassion is all
You know a cut hurts, don't you?
It hurts everyone

Yell hate at a child
Like yelling in a canyon
Expect an echo

Like blades to the soul
Words can be blunt or knife-edged
Choose them with real care

You're inferior
To no-one, nothing, never
Inferior none

Our fear and anger
Come from the same place in us
Painful confusion

People like their fear
We feel so full and alive
Anger is the same

Can't think or reason
I lose my calm and patience
I must be angry

Where does patience go,
In a burst of fear-filled wrath?
Calm replaced by pain

Read more and speak less
More input and less output
Feeds your mind and soul

Don't say you are wise
This is to invite dissent
Be wise; be silent